This Belongs To:

____